3 AM Musings

Upasana Desai

BookLeaf Publishing

Presentation by *BookLeaf Publishing*

Web: www.bookleafpub.com

E-mail: info@bookleafpub.com

ISBN: 9789357617864

First edition 2022

This book is dedicated to that one kid that often feels left out at family gatherings. Just know that people are lowkey jealous of your weirdness because it allows you to perceive the world differently.

Stay weird.

PREFACE

Most of the poems in this book have elements of myself in them. Growing up, writing was my outlet and as someone with an imagination that was always bigger than life itself. I often found myself sprawled by the beach with a good book or hunched over a laptop typing frivolously at odd hours of the night.

And this book is the outcome of my 3 AM musings. It is an insight into my world with the rawest of emotions etched across these pages.

So as you continue to ingest the book, my hope is that it will bring out some element of creativity. Within you. The reader. Because even in the messiest of moments I've always found that words helped me find my place in the world and I hope it does the same for you.

Home

Raised voices and shattered glass make their
way across the room.
I feel the blood rush to my face.
My jaw is clenched and I bite my tongue in a
futile attempt to calm the noise in my mind.

The sun settles behind the clouds and I taste
blood.
Metallic yet sweet.
His fingers wrap around mine. Tightly. So as to
remind me of my place in the world.
He says words that are inexcusable.
They rip into my soul and I immediately see red.
But then those same fingers pull me close and
those same lips tell me that they love me.
The red slowly fades into a soft pink.

I should walk away.
But how can I?
When this environment feels so familiar.
When it feels like home.

Purpose

My writing is my art.
It paints a picture of my soul.
The very depths of who I am are encased in the words that I write.

So when you ask me to tell you more about who I am.
I respond by saying.
Pay attention to the verbs. The punctuation. The nouns.
But more important pay attention to the grammatical errors.
Because they are a true encapsulation of who I am.

Even in my darkest moments, the words will find me.
Demand my attention until I give in.
Knock on my door like a stubborn child that will not leave until she gets what she wants.
Of course, in those moments I refuse to give her any attention.
After all stubborn recognises stubborn.

But then when the moon comes out to play.

And I can't drown out the voices any longer.
I find myself feverishly typing into my keyboard, as the world around me falls deep within its REM cycle.
Because even if I wanted to ignore her.
The universe would never allow it.

After all, she calls out to me and reminds me.
That it is my duty to serve a larger purpose.
She reminds me of my identity and provides me with a liberation so high that no drug could ever compete.
She reminds me that I am free to choose how I move in this world.

And that storytelling is my purpose.

Soulmate

Another evening spent in the arms of a stranger.
Another morning spent washing the regret off my skin.
As days slowly turn into years, I let strangers make themselves at home.
Hoping to find answers in their silence.
And comfort in their embrace.

Time after time I put my heart out on the line.
I love the thrill of it all.
Crave it like an unhealthy addiction.

And so I find myself staring at the cards in front of me.
Promising the stranger across the table an evening of adventure.
And at that moment my intuition tries to warn me. But I never dare to walk away from a promise that I make to a stranger.
Even if it means breaking a promise that I'd once made to myself.

The promise that I would always pour into myself first.

The promise that I would walk away from
soul-altering experiences if it meant the love that
I so deeply yearned for. Slowly started to
shape-shift into danger.

Sometimes in the quiet hours of the evening.
I wonder if I would've broken all those promises.
If I had been taught to harness the power of
solitude.
If I'd been told that in order to find my soulmate.
All I had to do was look in the mirror.

Seductress

She will ghost you when you least expect it.
Lure you into a dark corner and tempt you with promises that you know are too good to be true.
Each time you will tell yourself to walk away because everyone will warn you that nothing good happens after 2 a.m.

Yet you will find yourself in her embrace.
Lips locked together so feverishly that you will almost forget to come up for air.
But when you finally make the mistake of doing so, you will turn around and she is nowhere to be found.

In the blink of an eye. She will disappear.
And at that moment you promise yourself.
Never again.
Knowing deep down that if you ever were so lucky to have her beckon you over.
You would drop everything in a heartbeat and be at her mercy.

Because creativity is so enticingly rare.
That when she does beckon.
You can't help but listen.

Alive

I want to be thrown into a parallel universe
where uncertainty is embraced.
The kind where you have no idea what the future
looks like.
But you feel a sense of anticipation.
A tinge of fear.
But most importantly.
You feel alive again.

Delusional

I bet if you spent 24 hours inside my head.
You'd spiral.
One minute I'm feeling on top of the world.
The next I'm curbing the urge to get inked just so I can feel something.

One minute I'm commuting to work like your average joe.
The next I'm signing a dotted line before jumping out of a plane.

One minute I'm letting the wind play with my hair.
The next I'm curled up in a corner trying to focus on my breathing.

My therapist tells me that if I take it one day at a time.
One moment at a time.
The universe will unfold my path for me.
A path that was painstakingly embroidered by god himself.

So I close my eyes and do something that never comes easily to me.

I let go.
I let the universe hold the reins and leave it up to fate.

Some call it crazy. Delusional even.
But over time I realise that it takes strength.
To show up every day and believe that something larger than life will guide you.
Protect you.
It takes courage to believe in something intangible.
In a world that has brainwashed you into believing otherwise.

Friendships

There is something magical about female friendships.
They build you up in ways that almost seem mystical.
They make room for you to grow.
To heal.

They nurture your soul and fuel your fire.
They bring out the adventurous side in you.
They fill your cup when you feel like all that is left of you are the remnants.

They find the scattered pieces and build you back up.
So you make it through another day.
That is the kind of strength that can only be found in soulful female friendships.

Audacity

I wonder who led me to believe that I am too
picky.
When I refused to shrink myself in their
presence.

I wonder who let me believe that I had to act
foolish.
In order to make them feel empowered.

I wonder when I was conditioned into thinking
that my voice didn't matter.
Because I was being too naive by listening to my
intuition.

Jaded

I work myself to the core because the world
promises me luxury bags in exchange.
Instead, I'm left with the bags under my eyes.

I force myself into believing that being
productive is the only way to live.
When I'd much rather be basking in the rays of a
sunset.

I let capitalism wrap her freshly manicured
hands around me.
Until it gets so hard to breathe that I have no
choice but to give in.

So I tell her I will agree to her terms and
conditions.
As long as she gives me the stability I so deeply
yearn for.
The stability that I never had growing up.

She agrees.

And in that moment, I trade in my childhood
ambitions.

Never once questioning if any of this was my
true calling.
Or if I was simply jaded.

Survival

No one tells you that growing up as an
immigrant in a foreign country will put you in a
permanent state of flight or fight.
No one warns you, that you will have to work
twice as hard just so you are considered for a
seat at the table.
No one gestures towards the fine print, which
states that you will have to build a second
identity to fit into a system that was never built
to support people like us.

Sometimes in the brief moments of silence, I
find myself wondering who I would be.
If I wasn't in constant survival mode.

Addicted

We were all fed a lie.
Line by line.
The world convinced us into believing that when we get married we will be happy.
When we get that promotion we will be happy.
When we get that ring we will be happy.
When we have the largest home on the block we will be happy.

Line by line, over the years we were fed these lies.
And before we knew it. We were hooked.
Hooked on trying to achieve the next big goal.

But what they didn't tell us, was that at some point, each achievement was going to have to be bigger than the previous.
In order for us to feel like we've accomplished something.

Connection

In a day and age where we are more attached to
the screens in our hands.
I wonder what would happen if we looked up
once in a while.

I wonder if we would actually find the
connection our souls so deeply crave.
But so foolishly try to find through a piece of
tempered glass.

Unlearning

It took years before I realised my priorities were all wrong.
I let the noise from the outside world dictate my actions.
I let the fear consume my goals.
Goals that made my heart sing.

It took years of unlearning.
Before I could look in the mirror and finally catch a glimpse of who I really was.

Uncomfortable

It took an entire decade before I realised the truth.
The truth that life happens in unplanned moments.
The moments when your mind is calm and your soul is rested.
The moments when you are forced to sit with your feelings.
The good. The bad. The uncomfortable.

Life unfolds when we embrace those moments and let them be.

It took me a decade to realise that the messiness of life was where the magic lay.

Fighter

The world will always project its expectations
on people like me.
People who were born with the urge to please
everyone but themselves.
It will break your spirit into a thousand tiny
pieces so you don't take up too much space.
So you will fit into this pre-defined mould that
has been bought about through years of
suppression.

But I come from a nation that has fought
suppression by digging deep into its warrior
spirit.
So I never quite understood why they were
surprised when I demanded that the world make
space for me.

Aging

I can't wait to trace my fingers through the
wrinkles caused by laughter.
I can't wait to find my first grey as proof that
I've moved into the next season.
I can't wait to trade the insecurities of my
twenties for the calmness of my forties and
fifties.
I can't wait to be in a place where I can tell the
younger version of myself about the upheaval
we caused.
The chaos we created.
The new pathways we paved by taking a chance
on dreams that others were too scared to act on.

I can't wait to share a cup of tea with you on the
porch and reminisce over the memories we
created.
To look back fondly on the upheaval we caused.
The chaos created.

Brave

If the devil hadn't waltzed into your life and
caused the upheaval that he had.
You would have never known what you were
capable of.
You would have never learned the power of
creating a new life from the leftover pieces of
what once was.

If the devil hadn't created obstacles so daunting.
You would've never experienced the power that
came with tearing them down.

If the devil hadn't pulled you away from
everything and everyone you'd ever known.
You would've never known just how capable
you were of thriving in the unknown.

Freedom

I didn't know I was shackled until I exhaled in
relief.
As though I was holding my breath too long.

I didn't know I was in a cage until I found
myself daydreaming of an alternate reality.
Where the expectations that come with being
born a woman were not thrust upon me.

I didn't know I'd let non-tangible expectations
smother my will to create.
Until I found myself staring at a blank page
struggling to cover it with art.
That was when I knew freedom came at a price
that surpassed the zeroes in my bank account.

But it was a price I'd pay in a heartbeat.

Peace

The thing about peace is that once you get used to it.
You crave it.
On a spiritual level.
On a molecular level.
On a mental level.
You will do anything in your power to hold onto it.

And in the rare moments that you come across anyone who threatens to take that away from you.
You withdraw so quickly.
That they are left questioning if you were a fragment of their imagination.

Adventure

To taste your surroundings through the
perception of another person.
To catch a glimpse of the life they've lived.
To walk down the trail of memories that shaped
them into the person standing in front of you.

Is such a privilege.
Such as honour.

That when I get asked, why I choose to spend
money travelling to the ends of the earth to
collect moments like priceless monuments.
All I can simply do is look them dead in the eyes
and ask.

Why wouldn't I?

Hopeful

Time after time, I find myself sitting across the table from yet another stranger.
Time after time, I find myself imagining what my life would look like with this acquaintance in it.
And for a brief moment as I inhale the crisp autumn breeze. I let myself daydream.
I let my imagination run wild and let her paint an image of a future with a classic white picket fence.

My head says not again.
But my heart says, maybe this time it will be different.

www.ingramcontent.com/pod-product-compliance
Lightning Source LLC
Chambersburg PA
CBHW062204160726
48282CB00027B/998
* 9 7 8 9 3 5 7 6 1 7 8 6 4 *